D0272625

QUOTES THAT EVERY **WOMAN** SHOULD LIVE BY

BY OUTSPOKEN WOMEN OF CHARACTER

First published in 2015 by Baker & Taylor UK Ltd,
Bicester,
Oxfordshire
OX26 4ST

This edition reprinted in 2015

© 2015 Susanna Geoghegan Gift Publishing
Collated by Michael Powell
Design by Milestone Design
Layout by Bag of Badgers
All rights reserved.

No part of this publication may be reproduced, stored in
a retrieval system or transmitted in any form or by any
means electronic, mechanical, photocopying, recording
or otherwise without the prior permission of the
copyright owner.

ISBN 978-1-910562-01-7

Printed in China.

INTRODUCTION

Every day the world bombards us with advice, mostly unwanted, from friends, parents, lovers and even strangers scrambling to share their preoccupations, prejudices and fears.

But did you know that the human brain – governed by the overriding imperative: 'Minimize danger, maximize reward' – is actually hardwired to mistrust advice?

Thankfully, this book is brimming with comical counsel you'll be delighted to read and maybe even to follow. It's a collection of funny and occasionally helpful lifestyle suggestions, all from women. You won't find a single man among these pages because what do they know, right girls?

THE MAIN PURPOSE OF CHILDREN'S PARTIES IS TO REMIND YOU THAT THERE ARE CHILDREN MORE AWFUL THAN YOUR OWN.

KATHERINE WHITEHORN

SELF RESPECT IS FILLING THE BRITA EVEN WHEN YOUR ROOMMATE'S OUT OF TOWN.

SHELBY FERO

I get those maternal feelings; like when I'm laying on the couch and I can't reach the remote control.

KATHLEEN MADIGAN

I'VE DISCOVERED THE SECRET OF TIME TRAVEL; JUST WALK EVERYWHERE SLIGHTLY QUICKER.

GRÁINNE MAGUIRE

STUPID MEN ARE THE ONLY ONES WORTH KNOWING AFTER ALL.

JANE AUSTEN

Don't spend time beating on a wall, hoping to transform it into a door.

COCO CHANEL

IF MY LIFE FLASHES BEFORE MY EYES, IT'S MOSTLY GOING TO BE A MONTAGE OF ME AVOIDING PEOPLE I KNOW ON THE STREET.

APARNA NANCHERLA

I WANT MY NAILS DONE IN THE MIDDLE OF A CROWDED DEPARTMENT STORE AS MUCH AS I WANT MY SMEAR TEST DONE AT THE DUMP.

ALICE WHITE

NEVER DRINK BLACK COFFEE AT LUNCH; IT WILL KEEP YOU AWAKE ALL AFTERNOON.

JILLY COOPER

THE CHIEF EXCITEMENT IN A WOMAN'S LIFE IS SPOTTING WOMEN WHO ARE FATTER THAN SHE IS.

HELEN ROWLAND

Please don't ask me what something means or who someone is from your device which has access to the internet.

JENNY JOHNSON

I LOVE PUNCHING THE CEILING WITH MY FISTS WHEN I'M LOST OR I CAN'T FIND A PARKING SPACE.

LAURA KIGHTLINGER

A MAN'S GOT TO DO WHAT A MAN'S GOT TO DO. A WOMAN MUST DO WHAT HE CAN'T.

RHONDA HANSOME

I WANT MY CHILDREN TO HAVE EVERYTHING I COULDN'T AFFORD AND THEN I WANT TO MOVE IN WITH THEM.

PHYLLIS DILLER

Whenever I see the words 'Positive Discrimination', my lady brain magically turns it into 'Reversal of Prejudice'. Try it – it's fun.

KATY BRAND

PARIS IS ALWAYS A GOOD IDEA.

AUDREY HEPBURN

THERE'S MORE TO LIFE THAN CHEEK BONES.

KATE WINSLET

HEY LADIES WITH THOSE SEE-THROUGH BRA STRAPS! YOU KNOW WE CAN SEE THEM, RIGHT?

WENDY WASON

Whenever I put on my black leather gloves I do it with flair, like I'm about to go strangle someone on an episode of Murder She Wrote.

SAMANTHA BEE

I KEEP MY OWN PERSONALITY IN A CUPBOARD UNDER THE STAIRS AT HOME SO THAT NO ONE ELSE CAN SEE IT OR NICK IT.

DAWN FRENCH

I REALLY NEED TO STOP BEING SO PROUD OF MYSELF FOR REHEATING A PIECE OF LASAGNE IN THE OVEN INSTEAD OF THE MICROWAVE.

MORGAN MURPHY

CARPE SCROTUM. SEIZE LIFE BY THE TESTICLES.

ROWENA CHERRY

Life is like one big Mardi Gras. But instead of showing your boobs, show people your brain, and if they like what they see, you'll have more beads than you know what to do with.

ELLEN DEGENERES

IT'S REALLY BEST NOT TO TELL PEOPLE WHEN YOU FEEL BAD. GROWING UP IS ABOUT KEEPING SECRETS, AND PRETENDING EVERYTHING IS FINE.

CAITLIN MORAN

PLAIN WOMEN KNOW MORE ABOUT MEN THAN BEAUTIFUL WOMEN DO.

KATHARINE HEPBURN

THE ROAD TO ENLIGHTENMENT IS LONG AND DIFFICULT, AND YOU SHOULD TRY NOT TO FORGET SNACKS AND MAGAZINES.

ANNE LAMOTT

Sometimes the only reason I leave my house is so when someone asks about my day I don't have to say 'Netflix and avoiding responsibilities'.

ANNA KENDRICK

MONEY MAY NOT BUY HAPPINESS, BUT I'D RATHER CRY IN A JAGUAR THAN ON A BUS.

FRANÇOISE SAGAN

MEN ARE MORE INTERESTING IN BOOKS THAN THEY ARE IN REAL LIFE.

MARY ANN SHAFFER

IF I HAD TO LIVE MY LIFE AGAIN, I'D MAKE THE SAME MISTAKES, ONLY SOONER.

TALLULAH BANKHEAD

Never be afraid to laugh at yourself – after all, you could be missing out on the joke of the century.

JOAN RIVERS

NOTE TO SELF: WHEN NOTICING FLYAWAY HAIRS, DO NOT USE LIP GLOSS AS AN 'ON-THE-GO' HAIR GEL.

DANICA McKELLAR

NEVER ACCEPT AN INVITATION FROM A STRANGER UNLESS HE OFFERS YOU CANDY.

LINDA FESTA

ANY GIRL CAN BE GLAMOROUS. ALL YOU HAVE TO DO IS STAND STILL AND LOOK STUPID.

HEDY LAMARR

Before posting a pic of a friend both parties should have to simultaneously turn separate keys to initiate the sequence.

RACHEL LICHTMAN

THERE ARE ONLY SO MANY APPS YOU CAN PLAY ON YOUR PHONE UNTIL YOU REALISE THAT LIFE IS MEANINGLESS.

JOSELYN HUGHES

IF SOMEONE ASKS YOU IF YOU'RE IN LINE WHAT THEY MEAN IS GET IN LINE BETTER.

KAREN KILGARIFF

TO SUCCEED IN LIFE, YOU NEED THREE THINGS: A WISHBONE, A BACKBONE AND A FUNNYBONE.

REBA McENTIRE

Anybody who doesn't make you feel good, kick them to the kerb. And the earlier you start in your life, the better.

AMY POEHLER

I AM VERY SHORT-SIGHTED, AND IF I DON'T LIKE A SITUATION I TAKE MY GLASSES OFF.

JENNY ECLAIR

THE PENALTY FOR SUCCESS IS TO BE BORED BY THE PEOPLE WHO USED TO SNUB YOU.

NANCY ASTOR

LET'S ALL GO AHEAD AND CHECK IN WITH THE LENGTH OF OUR TOE NAILS EVERY NOW AND AGAIN.

KRISTEN BELL

There are two kinds of people I don't trust: people who don't drink and people who collect stickers.

CHELSEA HANDLER

SOMETIMES IN THE AFTERNOON I'LL BUY MYSELF A CUP OF COFFEE AND SIT DOWN AND PRETEND THAT I'M AN ADULT HUMAN WOMAN SIMPLY TAKING TIME FOR HERSELF.

JENNY SLATE

SOMEONE JUST SAID 'YUK' WHEN LOOKING AT MY BREAKFAST. I AM OFFICIALLY HEALTHY.

SARAH MILLICAN

Girls. Never date a man who has a better décolletage and firmer bust in a V neck top than you.

GRACE DENT

DON'T PUT OFF TILL TOMORROW ANYONE YOU COULD BE DOING TODAY.

EMMA CHASE

FORGET ABOUT THE FAST LANE. IF YOU REALLY WANT TO FLY, JUST HARNESS YOUR POWER TO YOUR PASSION.

OPRAH WINFREY

ONE REASON I DON'T DRINK IS THAT I WANT TO KNOW WHEN I AM HAVING A GOOD TIME.

NANCY ASTOR

THE SECRET TO LIFE IS THAT THERE IS NO SECRET AT ALL AND YOU DON'T GET YOUR MONEY BACK.

FAITH HILL

If you're feeling down, just say: 'that pappardelle make me dance' in an offensive Italian accent.

KAT DENNINGS

PEOPLE DON'T WANNA HEAR ABOUT YOUR DIET. JUST SHUT UP, EAT YOUR LETTUCE AND BE SAD.

NICOLE BYER

LIFE IS NOT ONLY KNOWING WHAT YOU WANT BUT WHAT YOU'LL SETTLE FOR.

JOAN BENNETT KENNEDY

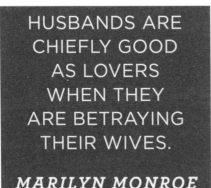

HUSBANDS ARE CHIEFLY GOOD AS LOVERS WHEN THEY ARE BETRAYING THEIR WIVES.

MARILYN MONROE

Make a sex tape, upload it, get on a reality show, release a perfume, retire. That's the new American dream.

NATASHA LEGGERO

I CAN GET READY IN 10 MINUTES.

CAROLINA HERRERA

NOTHING MAKES ME NEVER WANT TO DRINK AGAIN LIKE SEEING MY RECENTLY USED EMOTICONS.

WHITNEY CUMMINGS

Seriously, I don't need a gun. I'm easily annoyed. I would shoot people in my house that I invited over.

WANDA SYKES

THE SECRET OF STAYING YOUNG IS TO LIVE HONESTLY, EAT SLOWLY, AND LIE ABOUT YOUR AGE.

LUCILLE BALL

IF YOU'RE FEELING FLIRTY SUBTLY GRAZE A STRANGER'S ARM WITH YOUR FITBIT.

KRISTEN SCHAAL

DON'T THINK OF IT AS SHAVING, THINK OF IT AS 'HARVESTING LEG HAY'.

SAMANTHA BEE

THERE IS A SPECIAL PLACE IN HELL FOR WOMEN WHO DO NOT HELP OTHER WOMEN.

MADELEINE ALBRIGHT

Stars are not the people who are best at what they do; they are merely the people who want it most.

JULIE BURCHILL

NEVER, EVER GO TO BED WITH A MAN ON THE FIRST DATE. NOT EVER. UNLESS YOU REALLY WANT TO.

CYNTHIA HEIMEL

THERE IS NO GOOD AND EVIL, THERE IS ONLY POWER AND THOSE TOO WEAK TO SEEK IT.

J. K. ROWLING

IF THEY TURNED PROCRASTINATION INTO AN OLYMPIC SPORT, I WOULD DEFINITELY MEAN TO ENTER.

GRÁINNE MAGUIRE

I've never been married, but I tell people I'm divorced so they won't think something's wrong with me.

ELAYNE BOOSLER

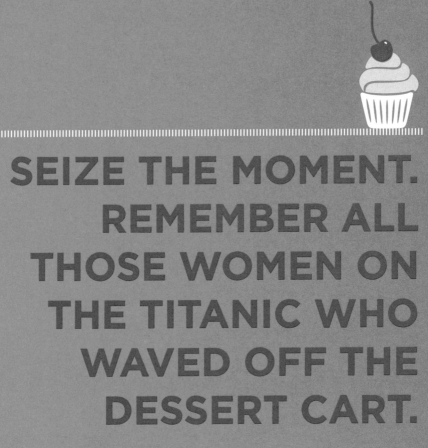

SEIZE THE MOMENT. REMEMBER ALL THOSE WOMEN ON THE TITANIC WHO WAVED OFF THE DESSERT CART.

ERMA BOMBECK

NEVER STRAY FROM THE PATH, NEVER EAT A WINDFALL APPLE AND NEVER TRUST A MAN WHOSE EYEBROWS MEET IN THE MIDDLE.

ANGELA CARTER

I always keep a wind chime next to the bed so I can brush my fingers across it as my lover climaxes.

MARY CHARLENE

WHEN LIFE SEEMS TO HAVE TURNED ITS BACK ON YOU, STAND UP AND KICK IT IN THE ASS.

KELLY LEBRUN

THE GREAT THING ABOUT BEING 39 IS YOU DON'T HAVE TO HAVE ANY OPINIONS ON MORRISSEY ANY MORE.

CAITLIN MORAN

I WANT A MAN WHO'S KIND AND UNDERSTANDING. IS THAT TOO MUCH TO ASK OF A MILLIONAIRE?

ZSA ZSA GABOR

YOU CAN TELL HOW SAFE A PARKING GARAGE STAIRWAY IS BY HOW STRONGLY IT SMELLS LIKE PEE.

JOSELYN HUGHES

Psychiatry is a waste of good couches; why should I make a psychiatrist laugh and then pay him?

KATHY LETTE

I REFUSE TO THINK OF THEM AS CHIN HAIRS. I THINK OF THEM AS STRAY EYEBROWS.

JANETTE BARBER

DON'T WORRY ABOUT WHAT PEOPLE THINK, THEY DON'T DO IT VERY OFTEN.

JACQUELINE DELISLE

CAN YOU IMAGINE A WORLD WITHOUT MEN? NO CRIME AND LOTS OF HAPPY FAT WOMEN.

NICOLE HOLLANDER

I've done the calculation and your chances of winning the lottery are identical whether you play or not.

FRAN LEBOWITZ

THERE MUST BE QUITE A FEW THINGS THAT A HOT BATH WON'T CURE, BUT I DON'T KNOW MANY OF THEM.

SYLVIA PLATH

I CAN'T UNDERSTAND WHY MEN MAKE ALL THIS FUSS ABOUT EVEREST.

JUNKO TABEI

It takes a lot of time to be a genius. You have to sit around so much, doing nothing, really doing nothing.

GERTRUDE STEIN

IF I HAD MY OWN RELIGION, ONE COMMANDMENT WOULD BE: THOU SHALT NOT BE RUDE TO WAITERS.

ST. VINCENT

I TRY BEING A VEGAN EVERY DAY, THEN CHEESE HAPPENS.

REBECCA CORRY

PART OF BEING YOUNG IS YOU THINK GAINING 6 LBS IS THE END OF THE WORLD.

MELISSA McCARTHY

ALL THE MEN WHO SEEM WORTHY OF MY LOVE ARE FICTIONAL AND WRITTEN BY WOMEN.

ERIN WHITEHEAD

Sex appeal is fifty per cent what you've got and fifty per cent what people think you've got.

SOPHIA LOREN

IF YOU CALL A CAT AND IT COMES RUNNING, WHAT YOU HAVE IS A DOG.

ARLINE BLEECKER

SOMEWHERE BETWEEN A SELFIE AND A PICTURE OF DESSERT LURKS A HEALTHY BODY IMAGE.

ANA GASTEYER

YOU HAVE A COUGH? GO HOME TONIGHT, EAT A WHOLE BOX OF EX-LAX. TOMORROW YOU'LL BE AFRAID TO COUGH.

PEARL WILLIAMS

If you have a burning, restless urge to write or paint, simply eat something sweet and the feeling will pass.

FRAN LEBOWITZ

IT WON'T BE LIKE THIS WHEN I RULE THE WORLD AND WE ALL FLY AROUND ON DRAGONS.

CAITLIN MORAN

HOMELESS PEOPLE DO NOT LIKE TO BE TICKLED. I REPEAT. HOMELESS PEOPLE DO NOT LIKE TO BE TICKLED.

JENNY JOHNSON

THE QUICKEST WAY TO KNOW A WOMAN IS TO GO SHOPPING WITH HER.

MARCELENE COX

When I'm hungry, I eat. When I'm thirsty, I drink. When I feel like saying something, I say it.

MADONNA

PEOPLE FORGET THAT CARS ARE GOOD FOR MORE THAN JUST TRANSPORTATION. THEY ARE THE PERFECT PLACE TO CRY AND EAT. YOU CAN EVEN DO BOTH AT ONCE!

NICOLE BYER

MY SECOND FAVOURITE HOUSEHOLD CHORE IS IRONING. MY FIRST BEING, HITTING MY HEAD ON THE TOP BUNK BED UNTIL I FAINT.

ERMA BOMBECK

ARE YOU SITTING COMFORTABLY? THEN GET UP. THIS IS NO TIME FOR SLOTH.

MAUREEN LIPMAN

If one of the activities in your 'busy day' is yoga, you are no longer permitted to consider yourself 'busy'.

SAMANTHA BEE

FOR ME, WHATEVER AGE OR SIZE I'VE BEEN, I HAVE RATHER LIKED MYSELF. THE SHELL IS NOT THE THING AT ALL.

DAWN FRENCH

I REFUSE TO CLEAN DISHES BEFORE PUTTING THEM IN THE DISHWASHER. GIVING MY APPLIANCE BENEFIT OF DOUBT.

JUNE DIANE RAPHAEL

IF YOU ACT CRAZY ALL YOUR LIFE, THEY'LL NEVER BE ABLE TO COMMIT YOU.

ROSEMARY SAUCIER

I don't understand people who make sex tapes; I can't even listen to my own voice on answer phones.

GRÁINNE MAGUIRE

NEVER KNOCK ON DEATH'S DOOR. RING THE DOORBELL THEN RUN. HE TOTALLY HATES THAT.

DARYNDA JONES

TO ME, THERE IS NO GREATER ACT OF COURAGE THAN BEING THE ONE WHO KISSES FIRST.

JANEANE GAROFALO

ACCEPT WHO YOU ARE. UNLESS YOU'RE A SERIAL KILLER.

ELLEN DEGENERES

I think how tan a person is, is directly proportionate to how dumb they are.

NATASHA LEGGERO

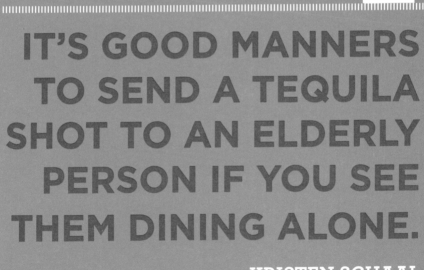

IT'S GOOD MANNERS TO SEND A TEQUILA SHOT TO AN ELDERLY PERSON IF YOU SEE THEM DINING ALONE.

KRISTEN SCHAAL

YESTERDAY I PINNED BACK A BAG OF FRIES TO MY PASSENGER SEAT WHEN I MADE A SUDDEN STOP AS IF THEY WERE A HUMAN. BEST DECISION I'VE EVER MADE.

JOSELYN HUGHES

I do not participate in any sport with ambulances at the bottom of the hill.

ERMA BOMBECK

WELL-BEHAVED WOMEN SELDOM MAKE HISTORY.

LAUREL THATCHER ULRICH

'NEVER LET THEM SEE YOU CRY.' I SAY, IF YOU'RE SO MAD YOU COULD JUST CRY, THEN CRY. IT TERRIFIES EVERYONE.

TINA FEY

PEOPLE WHO SAY THAT MONEY CAN'T BUY HAPPINESS JUST DON'T KNOW WHERE TO SHOP.

KATHY LETTE

Why on earth have I, because I'm a woman, got to be nice to everyone?

CAITLIN MORAN

IT HAS BEEN SAID THAT A PRETTY FACE IS A PASSPORT. BUT IT'S NOT, IT'S A VISA, AND IT RUNS OUT FAST.

JULIE BURCHILL

ONLY BUY CLOTHES THAT MAKE YOU FEEL LIKE DOING A SMALL DANCE.

HELEN FIELDING

CLEAR BRA STRAPS DON'T ACHIEVE THE GLAMOROUS LOOK THEY'RE DESIGNED FOR. YOU LOOK LIKE YOU'VE HAD A FIGHT WITH A SIX PACK OF STELLA.

LIZ BUCKLEY

ALWAYS BE A FIRST-RATE VERSION OF YOURSELF, INSTEAD OF A SECOND-RATE VERSION OF SOMEBODY ELSE.

JUDY GARLAND

Trying to look younger than you are is the number one cause of premature ageing.

SAMANTHA BEE

WHENEVER YOU FEEL SAD JUST WATCH ROBERTO BENIGNI WIN HIS OSCAR.

JENNY SLATE

BLOOD MAY BE THICKER THAN WATER, BUT IT IS STILL STICKY, UNPLEASANT, AND GENERALLY NAUSEATING.

JANEANE GAROFALO

'I'M DOWN!' I'M ADOPTING THIS PHRASE EVERY TIME I TRIP UP IN FUTURE.

RACHEL PARRIS

DO NOT, I repeat, DO NOT, put your money where your mouth is! There is poop on money!

EMILY HELLER

TAKE A NAP IN A FIREPLACE AND YOU'LL SLEEP LIKE A LOG.

ELLEN DEGENERES

I WOULDN'T KIDNAP A MAN FOR SEX, BUT I'M NOT SAYING I COULDN'T USE SOMEONE TO OIL THE MOWER.

VICTORIA WOOD

ALWAYS REMEMBER THAT YOU ARE ABSOLUTELY UNIQUE. JUST LIKE EVERYONE ELSE.

MARGARET MEAD

I named my boobs 'Rosh Hashanah' and 'Yom Kippur' because one's a slightly bigger holiday.

MEGAN AMRAM

IF YOU DON'T TAKE SELFIES, COOL . . . BUT YOU DON'T NEED TO GET ALL SELFIE RIGHTEOUS ABOUT IT.

ELLEN PAGE

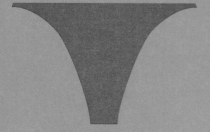

G-STRINGS ARE COMFORTABLE? THEY'RE NOT. THEY RIDE UP. BY THE END OF THE NIGHT YOU REALISE YOU'RE WEARING AN EYE PATCH.

KAREN BAYLEY

FIRST THINGS FIRST, SECOND THINGS NEVER.

SHIRLEY CONRAN

You don't always have to kiss a lot of frogs to recognise a prince when you find one.

JULIA QUINN

WE CAN TELL OUR VALUES BY LOOKING AT OUR CHEQUEBOOK STUBS.

GLORIA STEINEM

YOU CAN NEVER HAVE TOO MUCH BUTTER.

NORA EPHRON

SOMETIMES YOU JUST HAVE TO PUT ON LIP GLOSS AND PRETEND TO BE PSYCHED.

MINDY KALING

EMPTY WHAT IS FULL, FILL WHAT IS EMPTY AND SCRATCH WHERE IT ITCHES.

TALLULAH BANKHEAD

I don't trust anyone who seems okay with eating a bowl of cereal smaller than the size of their head.

SHELBY FERO

WHEN A MAN BRINGS HIS WIFE FLOWERS FOR NO REASON, THERE'S A REASON.

MOLLY McGEE

I LOVE PLANNING A MEAL WHILE EATING THE ONE BEFORE IT.

SARAH MILLICAN

It's okay to not be looking at what everyone else is looking at all of the time.

AMY POEHLER

ONE GOOD THING ABOUT BEING LOCKED IN A CAGE: NO RESPONSIBILITY!

KRISTEN SCHAAL

CHANCES ARE IF YOU HAVE MORE THAN ZERO BUMPER STICKERS ON YOUR CAR, WE'RE NOT GOING TO GET ALONG.

JOSELYN HUGHES

GOD'S ALWAYS GOT A CUSTARD PIE UP HIS SLEEVE.

MARGARET FORSTER

A TRUE FRIEND WILL GO WITH THE INSTAGRAM FILTER THAT FLATTERS YOU.

WHITNEY CUMMINGS

We all get given these bodies, and they're all fascinating and different . . . I wouldn't want to be without the wrinkles.

MIRANDA HART

I AM GOING TO STOP ALL MULTITASKING. I EVEN HATE THE WORD 'MULTITASKING'.

ELLEN BARKIN

WHEN A WOMAN BEHAVES LIKE A MAN, WHY DOESN'T SHE BEHAVE LIKE A NICE MAN?

EDITH EVANS

DOGS WITH HUMAN TEETH ARE NOT SELLING ME ANY PRODUCTS. NOT NOW, NOT EVER.

KAT DENNINGS

Ladies: remember to protect yourselves by deleting all the nudity from your bodies.

CAMERON ESPOSITO

WHEN LIFE GIVES YOU LEMONS, DON'T MAKE LEMONADE, MAKE PINK LEMONADE. BE UNIQUE.

WANDA SYKES

REMEMBER, IF YOU EVER NEED A HELPING HAND, IT'S AT THE END OF YOUR ARM.

AUDREY HEPBURN

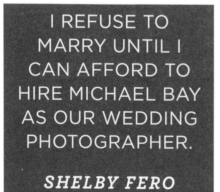

I REFUSE TO MARRY UNTIL I CAN AFFORD TO HIRE MICHAEL BAY AS OUR WEDDING PHOTOGRAPHER.

SHELBY FERO

You know you have a true friend when she wants to bail on the plans you made together exactly as much as you do.

CHRISSY TEIGEN

INSTEAD OF HAVING A BABY, WHY DON'T YOU GET A TATTOO OF A BABY FIRST, AND SEE HOW THAT WORKS OUT FOR SIX MONTHS TO A YEAR, AND THEN SEE IF YOU'RE READY TO HAVE A BABY.

CHELSEA HANDLER

FUNNY HOW WOMEN
ARE ASHAMED OF THEIR
INNER FAIRY WHEREAS
MEN ARE FOREVER
PROUDLY DISPLAYING
THEIR INNER COWBOY
OR FIREMAN.

DAWN FRENCH

THINGS ARE GOING TO GET A LOT WORSE BEFORE THEY GET WORSE.

LILY TOMLIN

My father always said, 'Be the kind they marry, not the kind they date.' So on our first date I'd nag the guy for a new dishwasher.

KRIS McGAHA

I HAVE CELLULITE PHOTOSHOPPED INTO EVERY NAKED PIC I SEND, JUST TO MAKE SURE HE'S IN IT FOR THE RIGHT REASONS.

KATHERINE RYAN

HEELS AND RED LIPSTICK WILL PUT THE FEAR OF GOD INTO PEOPLE.

DITA VON TEESE

EVERY MAN I MEET WANTS TO PROTECT ME. I CAN'T FIGURE OUT WHAT FROM.

MAE WEST

Sometimes you just gotta take a deep breath and say to yourself, 'Well, that part of my eyebrow is never going to grow back.'

LEAH BONNEMA

I'M REACHING CARTOON CHARACTER-LEVELS OF WEARING THE SAME JEANS EVERY DAY.

MEGAN AMRAM

PEOPLE SAY I'LL MEET THE MAN OF MY DREAMS WHEN I LEAST EXPECT IT. SO LIKE . . . WHEN I'M EMERGENCY POOPING AT A COFFEE BEAN & TEA LEAF?

MORGAN MURPHY

Hey celebs, if you don't want people looking at nude photos of you, maybe you should take some responsibility and stop having a physical form.

APARNA NANCHERLA

THE MOST COURAGEOUS ACT IS STILL TO THINK FOR YOURSELF. ALOUD.

COCO CHANEL

I DO WHAT IT SAYS ON THE ASPIRIN BOTTLE: TAKE TWO AND KEEP AWAY FROM CHILDREN.

ROSEANNE BARR

NEVER APOLOGISE FOR THE SPACE YOU TAKE UP IN THIS WORLD.

MARY CHARLENE

I WHISPER MY TEXTS ALOUD AS I WRITE THEM TO MAKE SURE THEY SOUND LIKE SOMETHING A NORMAL PERSON WOULD SAY.

KAREN KILGARIFF

As a rule, wearing a bigger pair of jeans looks better than squishing yourself into a pair of jeans that used to fit before you gave up smoking.

JENNY ECLAIR

WHEN IN DOUBT GO TO THE LIBRARY.

J. K. ROWLING

GIVE A GIRL THE RIGHT SHOES AND SHE CAN CONQUER THE WORLD.

MARILYN MONROE

IT'S NICE TO BE SHORT, BECAUSE PEOPLE EXPECT LESS FROM YOU.

AMY POEHLER

We get a lot of advice on how to improve ourselves from Instagram quotes when in reality the best way is to just get off our damn phones.

WHITNEY CUMMINGS

IF YOU'RE FEELING BAD ABOUT YOURSELF, JUST REMEMBER BRAD PITT MARRIED BILLY BOB THORNTON'S SLOPPY SECONDS. FEEL BETTER, HUH?

JENNY JOHNSON

YOU'RE ONLY AS GOOD AS YOUR LAST HAIRCUT.

FRAN LEBOWITZ

There is no such thing as conversation. It is an illusion. There are interesting monologues, that's all.

REBECCA WEST

IF YOUR DUDE HAS HIS HAND ON YOUR ASS IN YOUR ENGAGEMENT PHOTO I AM NOT COMING TO THE WEDDING.

EMILY HELLER

DIETS ARE LIKE BOYFRIENDS – IT NEVER REALLY WORKS TO GO BACK TO THEM.

NIGELLA LAWSON

LAUGHTER IS THE BEST MEDICINE, BUT THAT'S NOT TRUE IF YOU'VE GOT FACIAL INJURIES.

LINDA SMITH

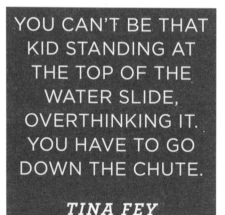

YOU CAN'T BE THAT KID STANDING AT THE TOP OF THE WATER SLIDE, OVERTHINKING IT. YOU HAVE TO GO DOWN THE CHUTE.

TINA FEY

There are two types of people in this world: people who say 'my birthday week' and people I wanna hang out with.

MOLLY McNEARNEY

JOGGING IS FOR PEOPLE WHO AREN'T INTELLIGENT ENOUGH TO WATCH BREAKFAST TV.

VICTORIA WOOD

WHENEVER YOU NEED TO WIN A SITUATION – TALK ABOUT JAZZ . . . IT CONFUSES PEOPLE.

CAITLIN MORAN

YOU CAN TELL A LOT ABOUT A PERSON BY THE THEATRICALITY OF THEIR COFFEE ORDER.

SAMANTHA BEE

The friend who holds your hand and says the wrong thing is made of dearer stuff than the one who stays away.

BARBARA KINGSOLVER

HAVE CHILDREN WHILE YOUR PARENTS ARE STILL YOUNG ENOUGH TO TAKE CARE OF THEM.

RITA RUDNER

HAVE ENOUGH SENSE TO KNOW, AHEAD OF TIME, WHEN YOUR SKILLS WILL NOT EXTEND TO WALLPAPERING.

MARILYN VOS SAVANT

I've got a Game of Thrones spoiler for you: you've got repressed sexual fantasies.

ALICE WHITE

JUST GO UP TO SOMEBODY ON THE STREET AND SAY 'YOU'RE IT!' AND JUST RUN AWAY.

ELLEN DEGENERES

IF YOU WANT TO KNOW WHAT GOD THINKS OF MONEY, JUST LOOK AT THE PEOPLE HE GAVE IT TO.

DOROTHY PARKER

WOMEN COMPLAIN ABOUT PMS, BUT I THINK OF IT AS THE ONLY TIME OF THE MONTH WHEN I CAN BE MYSELF.

ROSEANNE BARR

IF HIGH HEELS WERE SO WONDERFUL, MEN WOULD BE WEARING THEM.

SUE GRAFTON

Never trust anything that can think for itself if you can't see where it keeps its brain.

J. K. ROWLING

IF A MAN WATCHES THREE FOOTBALL GAMES IN A ROW, HE SHOULD BE DECLARED LEGALLY DEAD.

ERMA BOMBECK

DRUNK SWIMMING IS THE BEST. BECAUSE YOU'RE KINDA WORKING OUT AND YOU'RE DRUNK. KILLING SEVERAL BIRDS WITH ONE STONE.

NICOLE BYER

We can't be friends if you don't eat until you're physically uncomfortable.

MARY CHARLENE

CONFIDENCE IS 10 PER CENT HARD WORK AND 90 PER CENT DELUSION.

TINA FEY

I WILL NOT FOLLOW WHERE THE PATH MAY LEAD, BUT I WILL GO WHERE THERE IS NO PATH, AND I WILL LEAVE A TRAIL.

MURIEL STRODE

THE MORE DEVELOPED YOUR ABS, THE LESS TIME YOU'VE SPENT READING.

NATASHA LEGGERO

I KNOW ENOUGH TO KNOW THAT NO WOMAN SHOULD EVER MARRY A MAN WHO HATED HIS MOTHER.

MARTHA GELLHORN

I always cry at christenings. Thinking of all the better things I could be doing.

LIZ BUCKLEY

SHOW ME A WOMAN WHO DOESN'T FEEL GUILT AND I'LL SHOW YOU A MAN.

ERICA JONG

YOUR TRUE SELF IS REVEALED IN THE REFLECTION YOU SEE IN THE VENDING MACHINE.

ELIZA BAYNE

There's a reason the song doesn't go 'If you're happy and you know it, tweet at 1 am'.

EMILY HELLER

BLACK MAKES YOUR LIFE SO MUCH SIMPLER. EVERYTHING MATCHES BLACK, ESPECIALLY BLACK.

NORA EPHRON

I'VE NEVER HAD BOTOX. BUT I LIKE PEOPLE TO IMAGINE I HAVE.

JENNIFER SAUNDERS

I'M TOUGH, I'M AMBITIOUS, AND I KNOW EXACTLY WHAT I WANT. IF THAT MAKES ME A BITCH, OKAY.

MADONNA

CURVE: THE LOVELIEST DISTANCE BETWEEN TWO POINTS.

MAE WEST

I whisper 'you deserve this' to myself every time I turn on an air conditioner.

SHELBY FERO

KNOW THYSELF. DON'T ACCEPT YOUR DOG'S ADMIRATION AS CONCLUSIVE EVIDENCE THAT YOU ARE WONDERFUL.

ANN LANDERS

ANYONE ELSE WANT TO MAKE A RULE TO LIMIT HASHTAGS TO THREE PER POST? AND NO HASHTAGS THAT ARE SENTENCES?

WHITNEY CUMMINGS

NO ONE EVER DIED FROM SLEEPING IN AN UNMADE BED.

ERMA BOMBECK

Second, third and fourth chances are what it is all about.

ELLEN BARKIN

I CAN HAVE ICE CREAM IF I HAVE THREE PIECES OF FRUIT FIRST. MY NEW RULE.

SARAH MILLICAN

MEN WHO DRINK HERBAL TEAS ARE SELDOM SERIAL KILLERS.

RITA RUDNER

NEVER HAVE MORE CHILDREN THAN YOU HAVE CAR WINDOWS.

ERMA BOMBECK

To scare off a mountain lion, try to make yourself appear larger with your clothing, or just shout 'I LOVE YOU MOUNTAIN LION!' way too soon.

JULIEANNE SMOLINSKI

THE NEXT TIME A STRANGER IN A PUBLIC PLACE COUGHS HARD ENOUGH TO MOVE MY HAIR, THERE WILL BE CONSEQUENCES.

REBECCA CORRY

YOU DON'T NEED A SEARCH WARRANT TO GO THROUGH SOMEONE'S TRASH. SERIOUSLY. ONCE IT HITS THE KERB IT IS TOTALLY FAIR GAME – YOU CAN LOOK IT UP.

ALLY CARTER

NEVER EAT MORE THAN YOU CAN LIFT.

MISS PIGGY

If a man lies to you, don't get mad; get even. I once dated a guy who waited three months into our relationship before he told me he was married. I said, 'Hey, don't worry about it. I used to be a man.'

LIVIA SQUIRES

AT AGE 20, WE WORRY ABOUT WHAT OTHERS THINK OF US. AT 40, WE DON'T CARE WHAT THEY THINK OF US. AT 60, WE DISCOVER THEY HAVEN'T BEEN THINKING OF US AT ALL.

ANN LANDERS

A BIT OF LUSTING AFTER SOMEONE DOES WONDERS FOR YOU AND IS GOOD FOR YOUR SKIN.

LIZ HURLEY

IT'S BETTER TO DO NOTHING WITH YOUR MONEY THAN SOMETHING YOU DON'T UNDERSTAND.

SUZE ORMAN

It is my new short-term life goal to get ten sofas delivered before Christmas and pay nothing till the New Year.

ZOE LYONS

FRUIT IS NOT DESSERT. THE END.

SAMANTHA BEE

A CLEAN HOUSE IS A SIGN OF A MISSPENT LIFE.

JENNIFER KONERMAN

TO ATTRACT MEN, I WEAR A PERFUME CALLED NEW CAR INTERIOR.

RITA RUDNER

Listen to your kids, let them have opinions. If you don't, they'll turn into a-holes who argue with strangers in online comments sections.

JENNY JOHNSON

A WOMAN ESPECIALLY, IF SHE HAVE THE MISFORTUNE OF KNOWING ANYTHING, SHOULD CONCEAL IT AS WELL AS SHE CAN.

JANE AUSTEN

I ALWAYS PUNCH ART SCHOOL STUDENTS IN CASE THEY WOULD'VE BECOME HITLERS.

MEGAN AMRAM

IF YOU RETAIN NOTHING ELSE, ALWAYS REMEMBER THE MOST IMPORTANT RULE OF BEAUTY, WHICH IS: WHO CARES?

TINA FEY

Never purchase beauty products in a hardware store.

MISS PIGGY

EVERYONE'S ENTITLED TO MY OPINION.

MADONNA

THE THING WOMEN HAVE YET TO LEARN IS NOBODY GIVES YOU POWER. YOU JUST TAKE IT.

ROSEANNE BARR

I SHOULD BE SO LUCKY TO BE A MISFIT. I ASPIRE TO BE A MISFIT.

CLAIRE DANES

If you were born without wings, do nothing to prevent them from growing.

COCO CHANEL

THERE IS NOTHING LIKE PUKING WITH SOMEBODY TO MAKE YOU INTO OLD FRIENDS.

SYLVIA PLATH

LIGHTS ON, CURTAINS OPEN, SAT HERE NAKED EATING A WHOLE RAW PUMPKIN. BEST TRICK OR TREAT DETERRENT EVER.

ZOE LYONS

GOING TO THE DENTIST IS JUST LETTING A SUCCESSFUL PERSON PUT THEIR HANDS IN YOUR MOUTH. WHAT'S NOT TO LIKE?

ALICE WHITE

What doesn't kill us makes us funnier.

MARIAN KEYES

IT'S OKAY TO BE GOTH AT HEART.

KAT DENNINGS

NO WOMAN GETS AN ORGASM FROM SHINING THE KITCHEN FLOOR.

BETTY FRIEDAN

One sure way to lose another woman's friendship is to try to improve her flower arrangements.

MARCELENE COX

I FEEL LIKE NONE OF BUDDHA'S QUOTES TAKE INTO CONSIDERATION PMS.

ELLEN PAGE

A FRIEND NEVER DEFENDS A HUSBAND WHO GETS HIS WIFE AN ELECTRIC SKILLET FOR HER BIRTHDAY.

ERMA BOMBECK

WHEN CHOOSING SEXUAL PARTNERS, REMEMBER: TALENT IS NOT SEXUALLY TRANSMITTABLE.

TINA FEY

BETTER LATE THAN NEVER, UNLESS YOU WANTED TO BE PREGNANT.

LISA COFIELD

A balanced meal is whatever stays on the spoon en route to a baby's mouth.

KATHY LETTE

THE SQUEAKY WHEEL MAY GET THE MOST OIL, BUT IT'S ALSO THE FIRST TO BE REPLACED.

MARILYN VOS SAVANT

ON THE OFF CHANCE THAT YOU HAVE CHILDREN, DON'T CLEAN UP AT ALL. AS CHILDREN, MY BROTHER AND SISTER AND I LOVED WAKING UP EARLY AND PLAYING COCKTAIL PARTY WITH THE LEFTOVER DEBRIS.

AMY SEDARIS

No matter how closely you try to duplicate his mother's 'secret recipe' for pumpkin pie, yours will never be as good. His mother's 'secret recipe' for pumpkin pie can usually be found on the back of the can.

LISA COFIELD

NEVER TRUST A MAN WITH TESTICLES.

JO BRAND

WHEN MY PHONE SAYS 'SEARCHING', I HOLD IT TO MY HEART AND WHISPER 'ME TOO, PHONE, ME TOO', THEN BURST INTO TEARS.

LAUREN CALTAGIRONE

WHEN YOUR CHILDREN ARE TEENAGERS, IT'S IMPORTANT TO HAVE A DOG SO THAT SOMEONE IN THE HOUSE IS HAPPY TO SEE YOU.

NORA EPHRON

I THINK YOU LEARN MORE IF YOU'RE LAUGHING AT THE SAME TIME.

MARY ANN SHAFFER

Don't wreck a sublime chocolate experience by feeling guilty. Chocolate isn't like premarital sex. It will not make you pregnant. And it always feels good.

LORA BRODY

NEVER LOVE SOMEONE BENEATH YOUR LEVEL OF EVOLUTION. IF YOU WANT A MONKEY, YOU CAN VISIT ONE AT YOUR LOCAL ZOO.

SHANNON L. ALDER

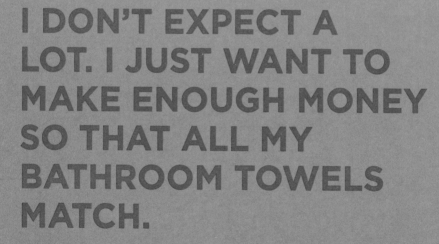

I DON'T EXPECT A
LOT. I JUST WANT TO
MAKE ENOUGH MONEY
SO THAT ALL MY
BATHROOM TOWELS
MATCH.

ADRIENNE IAPALUCCI

IF YOU CAN LAUGH AT IT, YOU CAN LIVE WITH IT.

ERMA BOMBECK

Do you want me to tell you something really subversive? Love is everything it's cracked up to be. That's why people are so cynical about it. It really is worth fighting for, being brave for, risking everything for.

ERICA JONG

AT THE END OF THE DAY, THE ONLY TRUE UNEQUIVOCALLY IMPORTANT ADVICE I CAN GIVE TEEN GIRLS IS: DON'T SEND NAKED PICTURES OF YOURSELF TO ANYONE.

MINDY KALING

IF YOU CAN'T BE KIND, AT LEAST BE VAGUE.

JUDITH MANNERS

THE ONLY WAY TO APPROACH MONDAY IS GET UP LATE AND THEN GO FOR A LOOOOOOOONG THREE-COURSE LUNCH AND THEN BEFORE YOU KNOW IT, IT IS TUESDAY.

ZOE LYONS

I always say to women, 'Take advantage of the fact that you're in the minority, don't see it as a disadvantage. You're that much more unique when there's fewer of you.'

CAROL LEIFER

ONLY TIME CAN
HEAL YOUR BROKEN
HEART, JUST AS ONLY
TIME CAN HEAL HIS
BROKEN ARMS
AND LEGS.

MISS PIGGY

ONCE YOU'VE KILLED A COW, YOU HAVE TO MAKE A BURGER.

LADY GAGA

All the mistakes I've ever made in my life have been when I've been drunk. I haven't made hardly any mistakes sober, ever, ever.

TRACEY EMIN

YOU JUST BE HONEST ABOUT WHO YOU ARE, AND IF YOU DON'T END UP WITH ANY FRIENDS THEN GOOD FOR YOU.

CHELSEA HANDLER

ONE OF THE SECRETS OF A HAPPY LIFE IS CONTINUOUS SMALL TREATS.

IRIS MURDOCH

OFTENTIMES 'EAT TOAST' IS THE ONLY SOLUTION MY BRAIN WILL OFFER.

KAREN KILGARIFF

IF HE WANTS BREAKFAST IN BED, TELL HIM TO SLEEP IN THE KITCHEN.

KATHY LETTE

Beware of men who cry. It's true that men who cry are sensitive to and in touch with feelings, but the only feelings they tend to be sensitive to and in touch with are their own.

NORA EPHRON

THE OLD THEORY WAS, MARRY AN OLDER MAN BECAUSE THEY'RE MORE MATURE. BUT THE NEW THEORY IS MEN DON'T MATURE. MARRY A YOUNGER ONE.

RITA RUDNER

IF IT HAS TYRES OR TESTICLES, YOU'RE GOING TO HAVE TROUBLE WITH IT.

LINDA FURNEY

Once you start making money, you can be an ass. But I am not an ass. I'm too lazy, that takes a lot of energy.

WANDA SYKES

NO ONE IS THINKING ABOUT YOU. THEY'RE THINKING ABOUT THEMSELVES, JUST LIKE YOU.

HELEN FIELDING

I WOULD NEVER JUDGE KATIE PRICE FOR THE WAY SHE GOES THROUGH HUSBANDS BECAUSE I'M EXACTLY THE SAME WITH HEADPHONES.

GRÁINNE MAGUIRE

STRENGTH IS THE CAPACITY TO BREAK A CHOCOLATE BAR INTO FOUR PIECES WITH YOUR BARE HANDS – AND THEN EAT JUST ONE OF THE PIECES.

JUDITH VIORST

Just because you're wicked smart it doesn't mean you are better than me.

AMY POEHLER

LIFE IS SOMETHING YOU DO WHEN YOU CAN'T GET TO SLEEP.

FRAN LEBOWITZ

WHATEVER WOMEN DO, THEY MUST DO TWICE AS WELL AS MEN TO BE THOUGHT HALF AS GOOD. LUCKILY, THIS IS NOT DIFFICULT.

CHARLOTTE WHITTON

FIRST RULE OF CLEAVAGE: IT'S NOT HOW LOW YOU GO, BUT WHERE AND WHEN YOU SHOW.

ELISABETH SQUIRES

If God had meant them to be lifted and separated, He would have put one on each shoulder.

VICTORIA WOOD

THE WORST PART OF SUCCESS IS TRYING TO FIND SOMEONE WHO IS HAPPY FOR YOU.

BETTE MIDLER